COWBOY MOVIE POSTERS

volume two of
the illustrated history of movies through posters

Published by BRUCE HERSHENSON
P.O. Box 874, West Plains, MO 65775

America's love affair with the Western film began in 1903 with the public showing of Thomas Edison's silent film *The Great Train Robbery*. Though not a shot was heard, the absence of sound did nothing to detract from audience enjoyment of this traditional tale of good versus evil. Officially declared dead as a doornail many times over, the Western has become the most enduring genre of American film. It continues to reload and come out shooting.

In the silent West of the early 1900s, men such as Broncho Billy Anderson, William S. Hart, and Tom Mix embodied Hollywood's vision of the cowboy hero. G.M. Anderson, a minor actor in *The Great Train Robbery*, later starred as hero Broncho Billy, adding this name to his own to become the first real cowboy star, Broncho Billy Anderson. William Surrey Hart, a stone-faced Shakespearian actor, often portrayed a badman whose love for a woman caused him to mend his ways. Hart's films, heavily laden with morals and manners, became hopelessly dated with the arrival of the roaring twenties.

Any real cowboy would have scoffed at the fancy duds of Tom Mix. This flamboyant cowboy was billed as the "Greatest Cowboy Star of Them All." His horse, Tony, was almost as popular and became the first in a long line of four-legged costars to receive second billing. Tom's on-and-off-screen persona won him a nation of adoring fans.

The great film director D.W. Griffith made well over 50 Westerns in the early years of the cinema, redefining the genre. He employed large casts, incorporated complex editing techniques, and developed more sophisticated uses of the camera. His early efforts paved the way for the epic film that would become so popular in the twenties.

The movie posters advertising these Western films made use of striking images to convey the thrills awaiting the ticket buyer. Posters promised a perfect afternoon with a favorite cowboy and grand visions of 'Hollywood's Wild West': white-Stetsoned buckaroos atop wild stallions, their guns drawn and blazing; runaway horses and careening stagecoaches; furious gun battles; and herds of stampeding steers.

Studio artists in charge of designing these posters were given free reign to let their imaginations run wild. In many cases, the poster art and the film's title had little to do with the actual movie, instead designed to boost theater attendance. Several artists worked on each poster, one handling the illustration work, one the typography, and another the design. Artists often specialized, some in faces, some in animals, and others in action scenes. In the early years of the cinema, posters were all-important to a film's success. Movies relied almost exclusively on the posters to bring in patrons. Poster art was often used to sell a film to theater chains before the movie was even made. The studios lacked today's complex programs for marketing a film...there was no television, no film review shows, and nowhere near the word of mouth promotion.

1 THE SQUAW MAN, 1907, theatrical poster (not a movie poster)

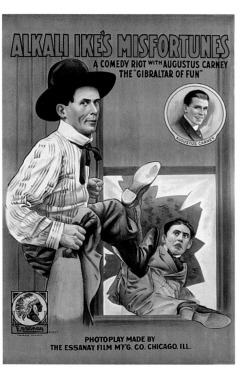

2 ALKALI IKE'S MISFORTUNES, 1913

3 THE CATTLE THIEF'S ESCAPE, 1913

4 THE ESCAPE OF JIM DOLAN, 1913

5 THE SPOILERS, 1914

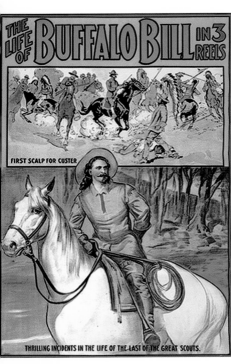

6 THE LIFE OF BUFFALO BILL, 1914

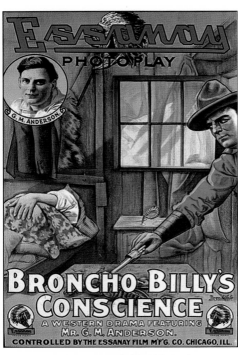

7 BRONCHO BILLY'S CONSCIENCE, 1915

8 THE CONVERSION OF "FROSTY"
BLAKE, circa 1915

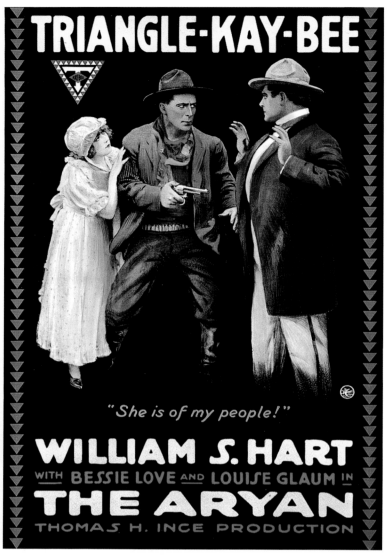

9 THE ARYAN, 1916

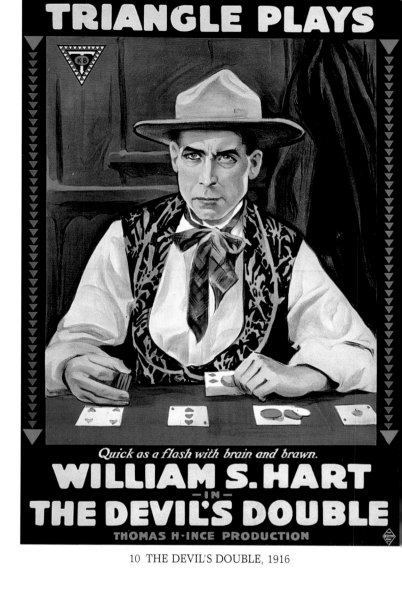

10 THE DEVIL'S DOUBLE, 1916

11 HELL'S HINGES, 1916, lobby card, 11 × 14 in

12 BLUE BLAZES' RAWDEN, 1918

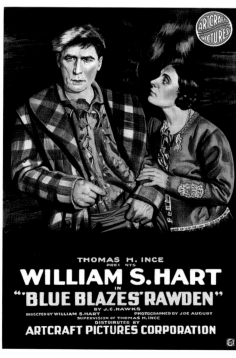

13 THE BORDER WIRELESS, 1918

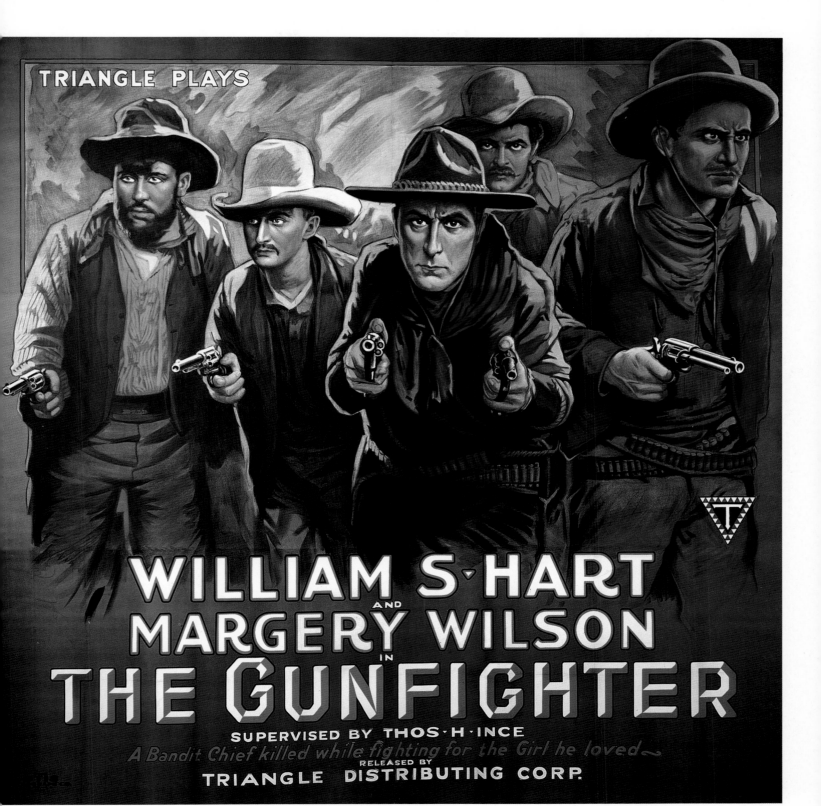

14 THE GUNFIGHTER, 1917, six-sheet,
81 × 81 in

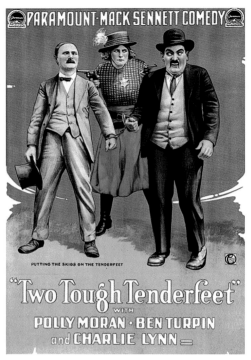

15 TWO TOUGH TENDERFEET, 1918

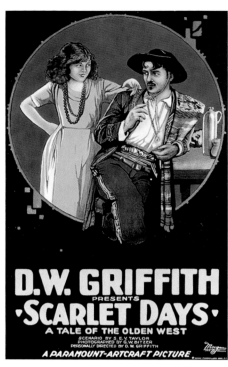

16 SCARLET DAYS, 1919

17 THE SPEED MANIAC, 1919

18 THE DEAD SHOT, 1918, three-sheet,
81 × 41 in

19 TEMPEST CODY RIDES WILD, 1919,
three-sheet, 81 × 41 in

20 THE CYCLONE, 1920, three-sheet,
81 × 41 in

The success of the Western film attracted many prospective cowboys to the Hollywood hills. The career of Tom Mix broke into a full gallop, while Ken Maynard and Buck Jones, who had appeared in bit parts in the Mix films, became stars in their own right.

Maynard, once a champion rodeo and circus trick rider, began his career in 1926 at First National. The films he made there are generally considered to be among the finest Westerns ever made. His horse, Tarzan, received second billing and trotted off with some of the better acting notices.

Buck Jones worked as a Wild West Show performer and horse trainer before becoming a world-famous cowboy star. He began as a stunt double, graduating to star in his own pictures in 1919. His long and successful film career ended tragically with his death in a nightclub fire in 1942.

Because they were excluded from most Hollywood films of the twenties, African-Americans began making their own films, including Westerns. Many were produced at the Norman Film Studio in Florida.

The big budgeted 1923 film *The Covered Wagon* was a blockbuster hit that cleared the trail for future large scale Westerns. An army colonel from the Wyoming Board of Indian Commissioners, Tim McCoy, was called in as advisor on the movie. McCoy became so fascinated with making movies, he signed with MGM the following year, beginning a 20-year career as one of the cowboy greats. Another epic followed in 1924, *The Iron Horse.* John Ford directed this railroad masterpiece, which launched the career of cowboy all-star George O'Brien. Ford worked as a film extra before becoming the dean of Western film directors. As he would do later with John Wayne, Ford used soft-spoken Harry Carey in many of his early films. Carey was more of an actor than a man of action. His long association with Ford provided him with many fine roles, and later he became a successful character actor.

Hoot Gibson had appeared in the Tom Mix films and doubled for Harry Carey. Gibson's good-old-boy characterizations earned him top cowboy honors at Universal Studios and kept him on the list of favorites for 20 years.

Other cowboy stars of the decade came and went with little fanfare. Among them were Jack Hoxie, one of Universal's biggest draws, and Art Acord, a champion bulldogger who could throw a steer in 24 seconds.

Near the end of the decade, something miraculous happened… movies began to talk. Movie houses soon reverberated with the sounds of gunfire, cattle stampedes and, for the first time, talking cowboys. Audiences thrilled when, in the 1929 "All-Talking" classic, *The Virginian,* Gary Cooper responded to Walter Huston's taunting "You long-legged son-of-a", with, "If you're going to call me that, smile."

21 3 GOLD COINS, 1920   22 HUMAN STUFF, 1920   23 TWO MOONS, 1920

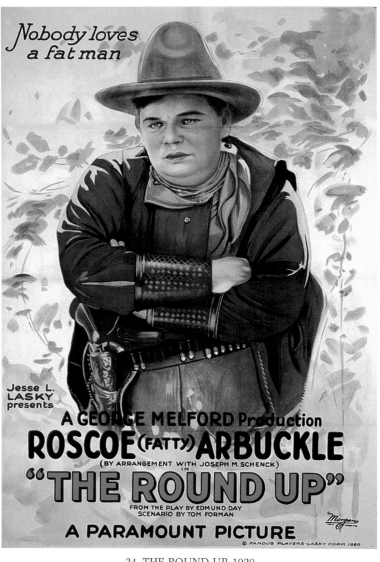

24 THE ROUND UP, 1920

25 THE MARK OF ZORRO, 1920

26 TEXAS GUINAN, 1920

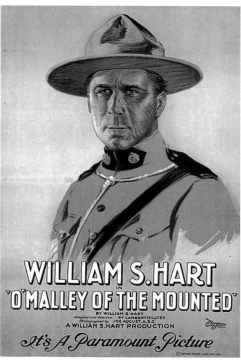

27 O'MALLEY OF THE MOUNTED, 1920

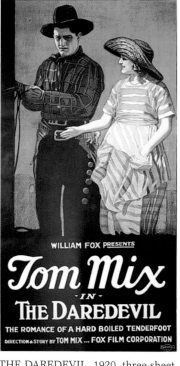

28 THE DAREDEVIL, 1920, three-sheet, 81 × 41 in

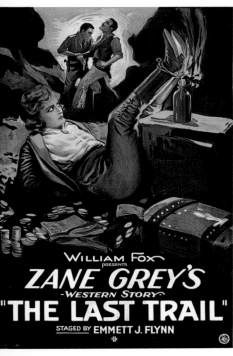

29 THE LAST TRAIL, 1921

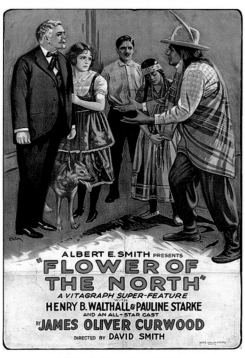

30 FLOWER OF THE NORTH, 1922

31 WHERE IS THIS WEST?, 1923

32 IN THE DAYS OF BUFFALO BILL,
CHAPTER 9, 1922

33 THE HALF-BREED, 1922

34 THE COVERED WAGON, 1923,
window card, 22 × 14 in

35 THE COVERED WAGON, 1923, insert,
36 × 14 in

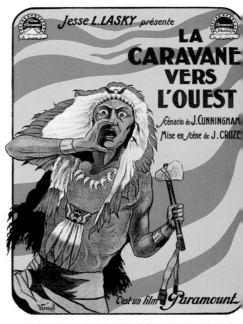

36 THE COVERED WAGON, 1923, original
French poster, 63 × 47 in

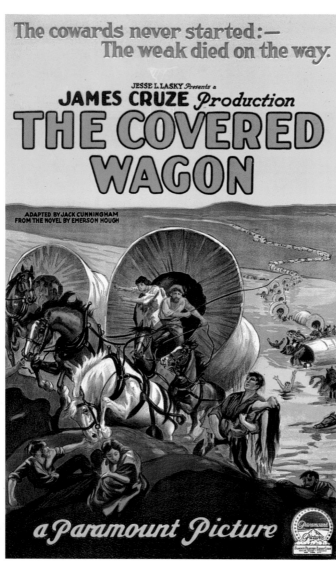

37 THE COVERED WAGON, 1923

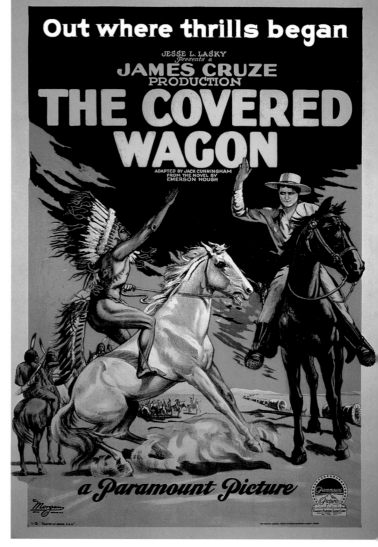

38 THE COVERED WAGON, 1923

39 THE CRIMSON SKULL, 1923, six-sheet
81 × 81 in

40 THE BULL-DOGGER, 1923,
three–sheet, 81 × 41 in

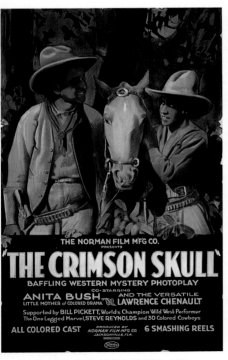

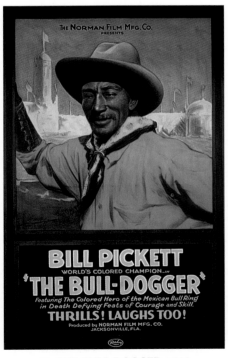

41 THE CRIMSON SKULL, 1923

42 THE BULL-DOGGER, 1923

43 FLAMING CRISIS, 1924

44 DEAD GAME, 1923

45 A DEBTOR TO THE LAW, 1924

46 THE LAST OF THE DUANES, 1924

47 THE IRON HORSE, 1924, lobby card,
11 × 14 in

48 THE BORDER LEGION, 1924

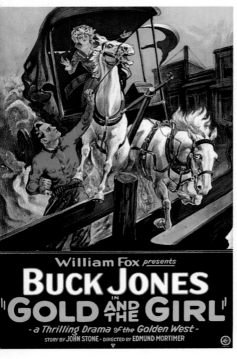

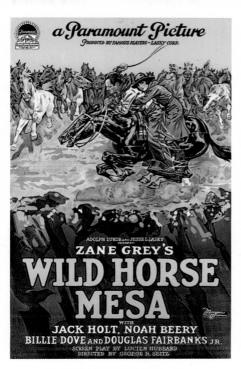

49 GOLD AND THE GIRL, 1925

50 WILD HORSE MESA, 1925

51 A WESTERN ENGAGEMENT, 1925

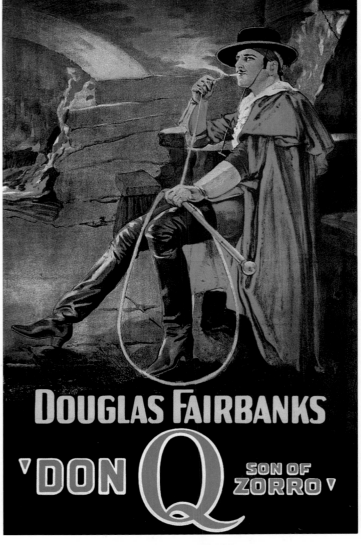

52 THE TRAIL RIDER, 1925

53 DON Q SON OF ZORRO, 1925

54 NO MAN'S GOLD, 1926

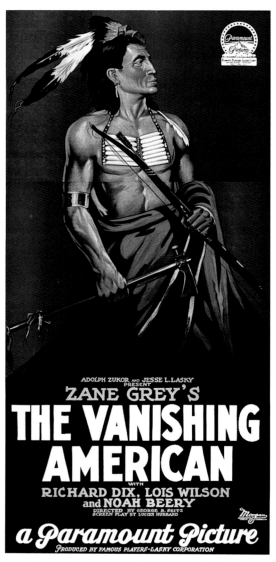

55 THE VANISHING AMERICAN, 1926,
three-sheet, 81 × 41 in

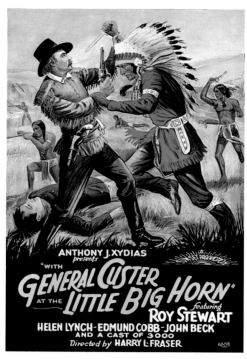

56 WITH GENERAL CUSTER AT THE
LITTLE BIG HORN, 1926

57 THE WINNING OF BARBARA
WORTH, 1926

58 THE TERROR, 1926

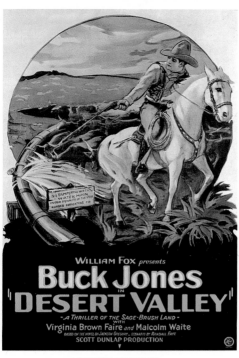

59 THE FLYING HORSEMAN, 1926

60 DESERT VALLEY, 1927

61 CHAIN LIGHTNING, 1927

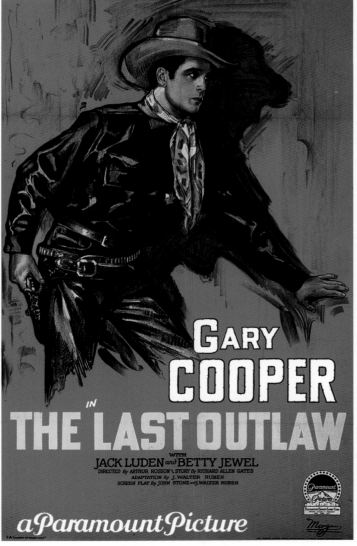

62 THE WAGON SHOW, 1927

63 THE LAST OUTLAW, 1927

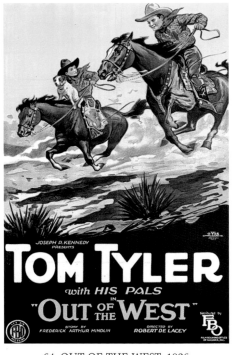

64 OUT OF THE WEST, 1926

65 MEN OF DARING, 1927

66 SILVER VALLEY, 1927

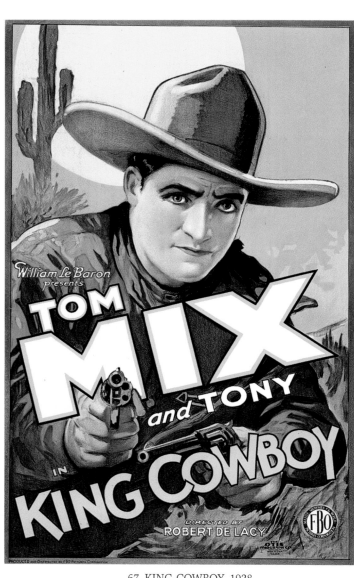

67 KING COWBOY, 1928

68 THE COWBOY KID, 1928

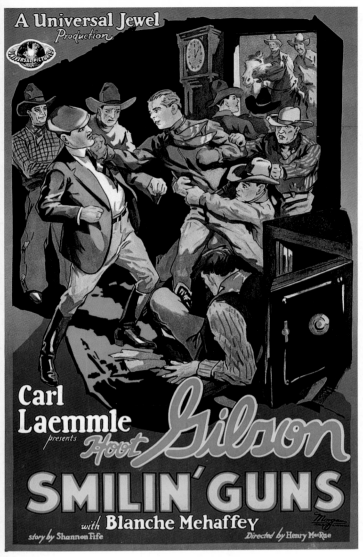

69 SMILIN' GUNS, 1928

70 THE TRAIL OF '98, 1929

71 AVALANCHE, 1928

72 SON OF THE GOLDEN WEST, 1928

73 GUN LAW, 1929, three-sheet, 81 × 41 in

74 THE VIRGINIAN, 1929

75 IN OLD ARIZONA, 1929

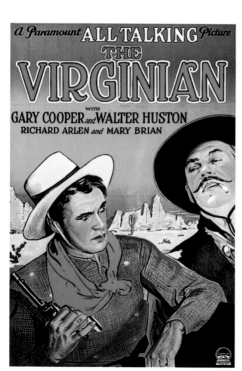

76 THE VIRGINIAN, 1929

77 THE VIRGINIAN, 1929, insert,
36 × 14 in

78 BOB STEELE, circa 1930, three-sheet,
81 × 41 in

The thirties were a magical time in movie history. The best talents from around the world assembled in Hollywood to make great motion pictures, many of them Westerns.

The movies were talking now, and the filmgoing public turned out in droves to experience this new phenomenon. Not all theaters were equipped to handle sound, so both a silent and a sound version of a film were often released. The earliest 'sound' films consisted of little more than sound effects with a few scattered lines of dialogue.

In 1930, director Raoul Walsh gave an inexperienced actor the lead role in his epic wagon-train film, *The Big Trail*. It was not well received, and its star, John Wayne, seemed destined for obscurity. Wayne moved to Vitagraph, where he made several films for Warner Brothers cartoon king, Leon Schlesinger. These films were built around footage taken from Ken Maynard's silent First National films, with Wayne dressed in outfits identical to Maynard's and the scenes carefully matched.

Cimarron, a large-scale Western tale of the Oklahoma land rush, lassoed the Oscar for best picture in 1930. Its star, Richard Dix, continued to work in grand-scale Westerns for the next 20 years.

Though Gene Autry is generally credited with being the first singing cowboy, it was the early Ken Maynard talkies that introduced musical interludes to the Western. Maynard sang and accompanied himself on the guitar, fiddle, or accordion, and later wrote the theme songs for many of his films. In 1934, Gene Autry performed several musical numbers in the Maynard film, *In Old Santa Fe*. Later, Autry replaced Maynard as star of the Science-Fiction Western serial, *The Phantom Empire*. So began the legendary career of the singing cowboy.

Columbia Pictures, after securing the talents of Buck Jones and Tim McCoy, gave top priority to their new Western series. Many of the finest cowboy films and cowboy posters were produced at Columbia. The studio artists designed fantastic portrait-style posters of their Western stars. A good example is the art deco "Marlboro Man" poster from the 1932 Buck Jones film, *Ridin' For Justice*.

Some cowboy stars found the microphone to be a career stopper, but most of the major silent stars had some degree of success in talkies.

In 1932, Tom Mix briefly came out of retirement to star in a high-quality series of films for Universal. Tom Tyler, silent cowboy star, was perfectly suited for the talkies with his deep, rich voice. Unfortunately, he was saddled with poor scripts and low budgets for the remainder of his career. Bob Steele was a small, feisty cowboy star who continued to give good performances in low-budget films throughout his long career. He often appeared in films written and directed by his father, Robert N. Bradbury. George O'Brien continued to star in high-quality cowboy movies throughout the thirties.

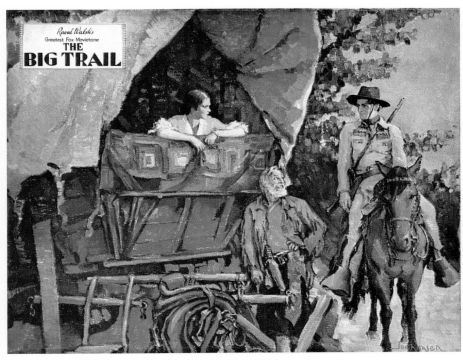

79 THE BIG TRAIL, 1930, lobby card,
11 × 14 in

80 THE BIG TRAIL, 1930, window card,
22 × 14 in

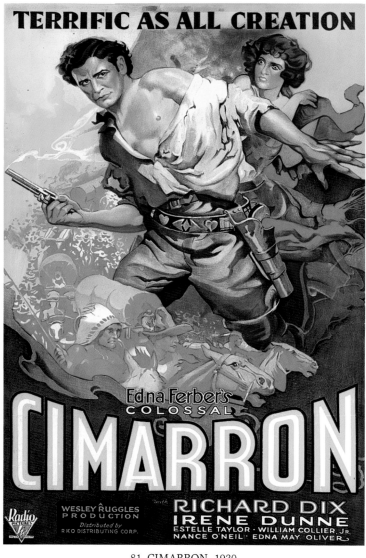

81 CIMARRON, 1930

82 CIMARRON, 1930, original Swedish poster, 41 × 27 in

83 THE FIGHTING LEGION, 1930

84 BAR L RANCH, 1930

85 FAIR WARNING, 1930

86 ROMANCE OF THE WEST, 1930

87 SPURS, 1930

88 SPURS, 1930

89 SONG OF THE WEST, 1930

90 THE SPOILERS, 1930

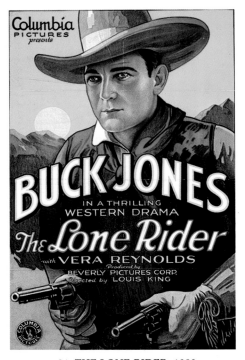

91 THE LONE RIDER, 1930

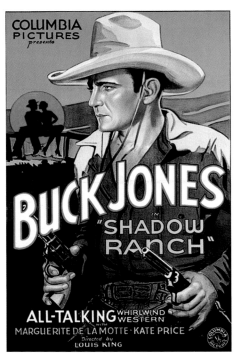

92 SHADOW RANCH, 1930

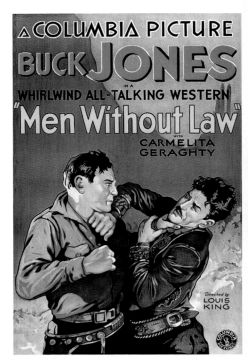

93 MEN WITHOUT LAW, 1930

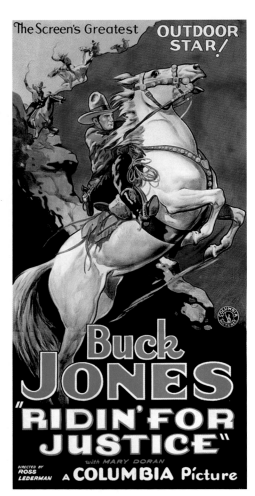

94 RIDIN' FOR JUSTICE, 1931, three-sheet, 81 × 41 in

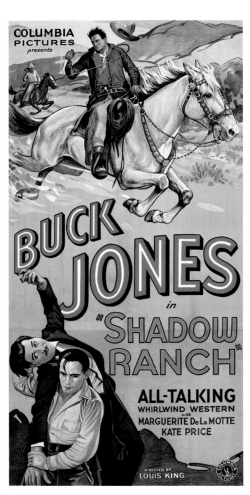

95 SHADOW RANCH, 1930, three-sheet, 81 × 41 in

96 BORDER LAW, 1931, three-sheet, 81 × 41 in

97 ONE MAN LAW, 1931

98 RIDIN' FOR JUSTICE, 1931

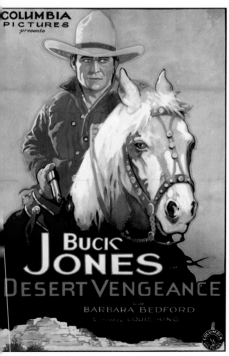

99 DESERT VENGEANCE, 1931

100 GUN SMOKE, 1931

101 THE RAINBOW TRAIL, 1931

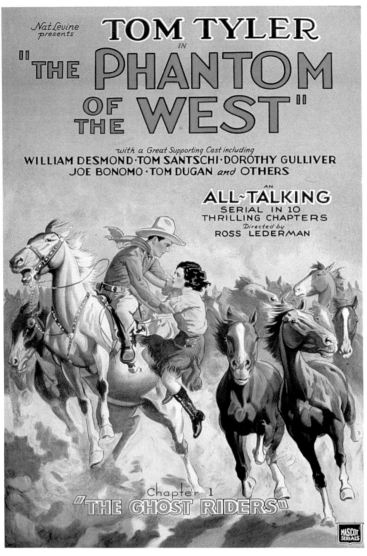

102 THE PHANTOM OF THE WEST,
CHAPTER 1, 1931

103 THE PHANTOM OF THE WEST,
CHAPTER 2, 1931

104 THE PHANTOM OF THE WEST,
CHAPTER 3, 1931

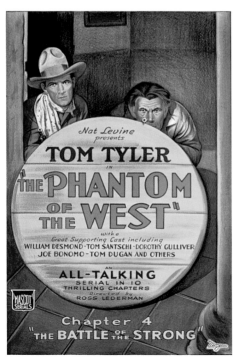

105 THE PHANTOM OF THE WEST,
CHAPTER 4, 1931

106 THE PHANTOM OF THE WEST,
CHAPTER 5, 1931

107 THE PHANTOM OF THE WEST,
CHAPTER 6, 1931

108 THE PHANTOM OF THE WEST,
CHAPTER 7, 1931

109 THE PHANTOM OF THE WEST,
CHAPTER 8, 1931

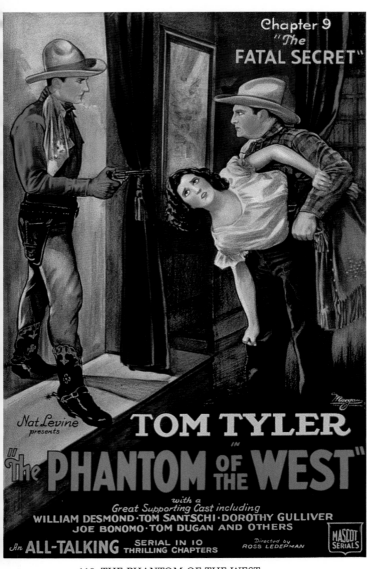

110 THE PHANTOM OF THE WEST,
CHAPTER 9, 1931

111 THE PHANTOM OF THE WEST,
CHAPTER 10, 1931

112 FIGHTING CARAVANS, 1931

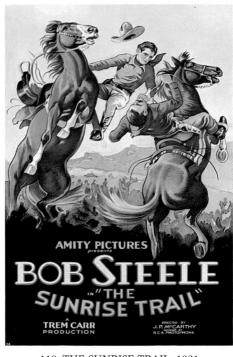

113 THE SUNRISE TRAIL, 1931

114 THE FORTY-NINERS, 1932

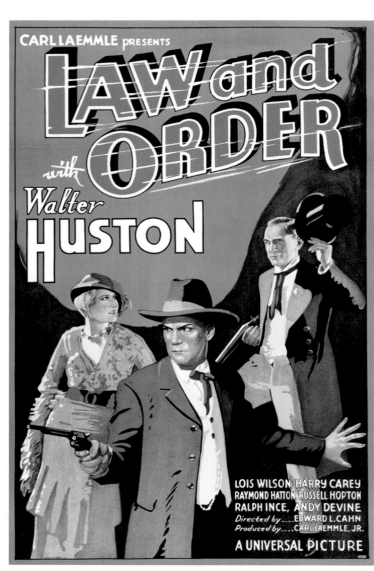

115 LAW AND ORDER, 1932

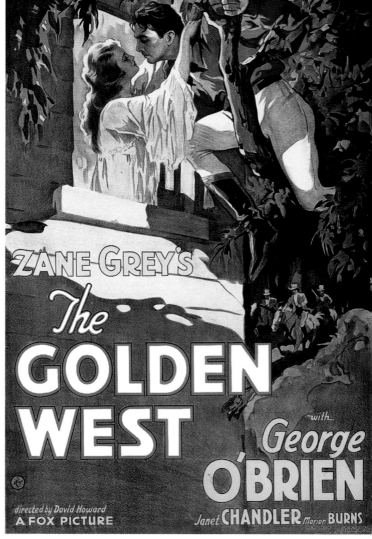

116 THE GOLDEN WEST, 1932

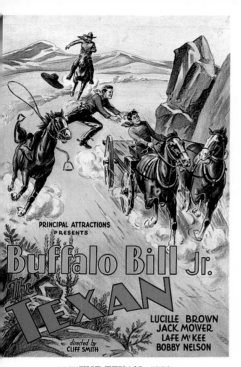

117 THE TEXAN, 1932

118 THE DEADLINE, 1932

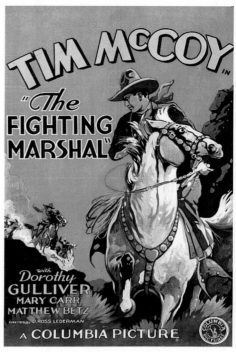

119 THE FIGHTING MARSHAL, 1932

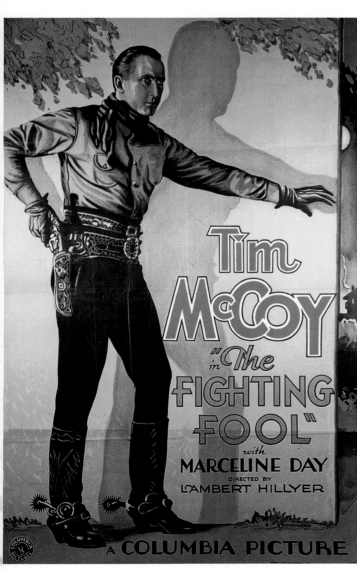

120 THE FIGHTING FOOL, 1932

121 SOUTH OF THE RIO GRANDE, 1932

122 CORNERED, 1932, three-sheet,
81 × 41 in

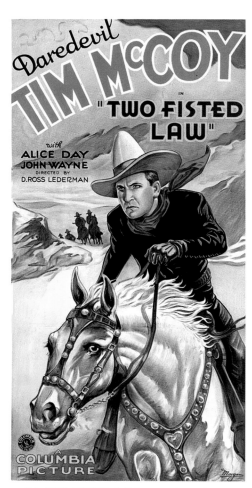

123 TWO FISTED LAW, 1932, three-sheet,
81 × 41 in

124 WHITE EAGLE, 1932, three-sheet,
81 × 41 in

125 CORNERED, 1932

126 TWO FISTED LAW, 1932

127 WHITE EAGLE, 1932

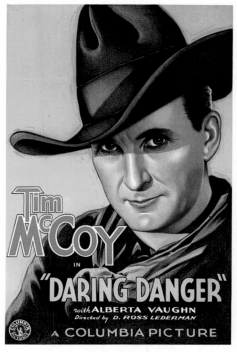

128 McKENNA OF THE MOUNTED, 1932

129 FIGHTING FOR JUSTICE, 1932

130 DARING DANGER, 1932

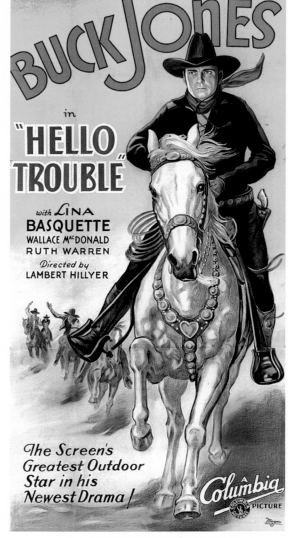

131 TEXAS CYCLONE, 1932

132 HELLO TROUBLE, 1932, three-sheet,
81 × 41 in

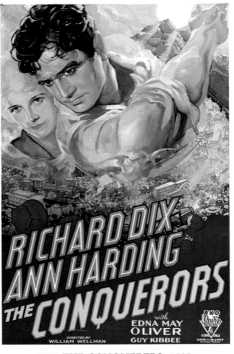

133 THE CONQUERERS, 1932

134 MY PAL, THE KING, 1932

135 PARTNERS, 1932

136 DESTRY RIDES AGAIN, 1932, three-sheet, 81 × 41 in

137 CAVALIER OF THE WEST, 1932, six-sheet, 81 × 81 in

138 SOMEWHERE IN SONORA, 1933

139 HAUNTED GOLD, 1933

140 DEADWOOD PASS, 1933

141 SON OF THE BORDER, 1933

142 THE MAN FROM MONTEREY, 1933

143 RUSTY RIDES ALONE, 1933, three-sheet, 81 × 41 in

144 RUSTY RIDES ALONE, 1933

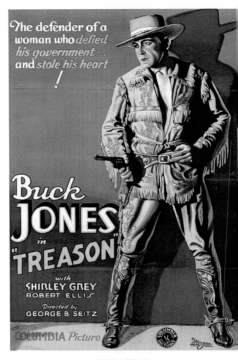

145 TREASON, 1933

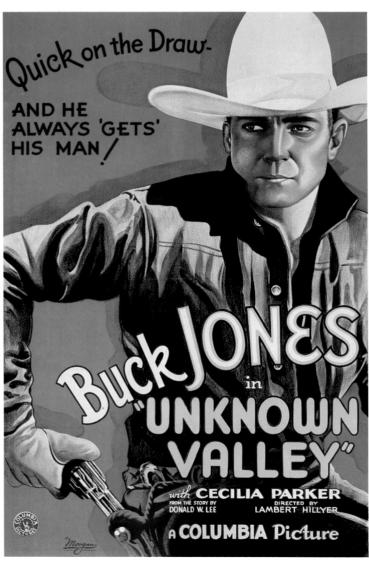

146 UNKNOWN VALLEY, 1933

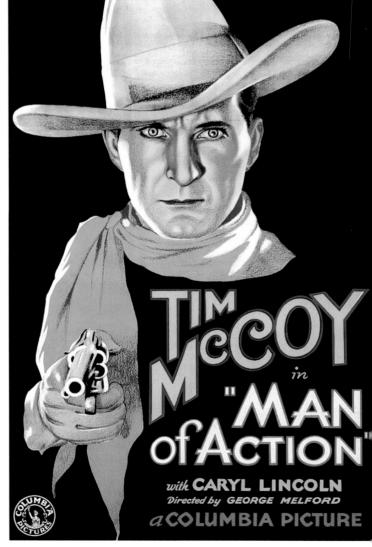

147 MAN OF ACTION, 1933

148 SILENT MEN, 1933

149 UNKNOWN VALLEY, 1933, three-sheet, 81 × 41 in

150 TRAILING NORTH, 1933

151 YOUNG BLOOD, 1933

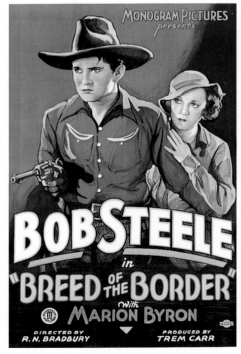

152 BREED OF THE BORDER, 1933

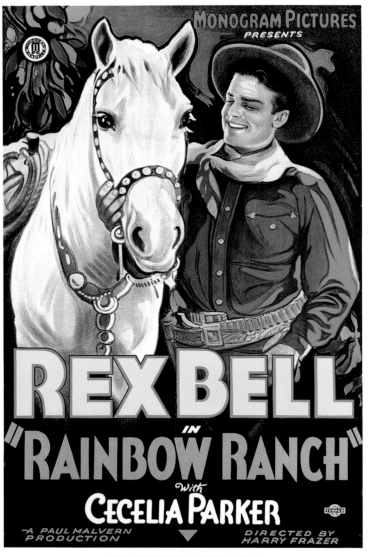

153 RAINBOW RANCH, 1933

154 DIAMOND TRAIL, 1933

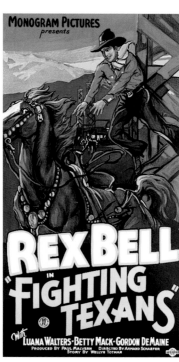

155 FIGHTING TEXANS, 1933, three-sheet, 81 × 41 in

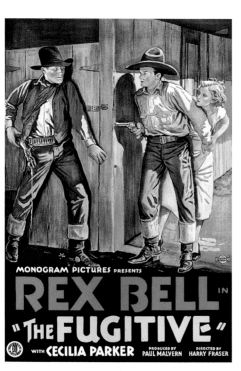

156 THE FUGITIVE, 1933

157 DIAMOND TRAIL, 1933, three-sheet, 81 × 41 in

158 SMOKY, 1933

159 SMOKE LIGHTNING, 1933

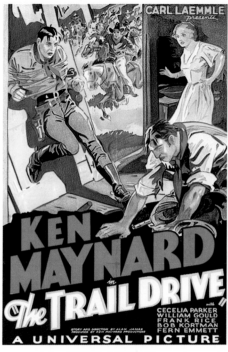

160 THE TRAIL DRIVE, 1933

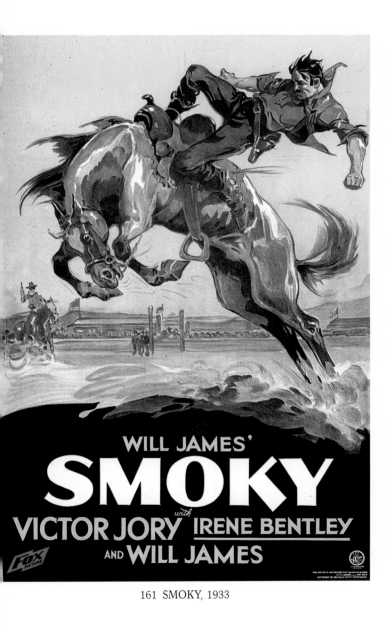

161 SMOKY, 1933

162 UNDER THE TONTO RIM, 1933

163 THE LAST ROUND-UP, 1934

164 WAGON WHEELS, 1934

165 FRONTIER MARSHAL, 1934

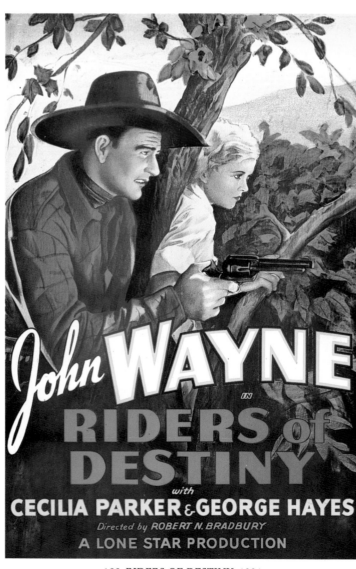

166 RIDERS OF DESTINY, 1934

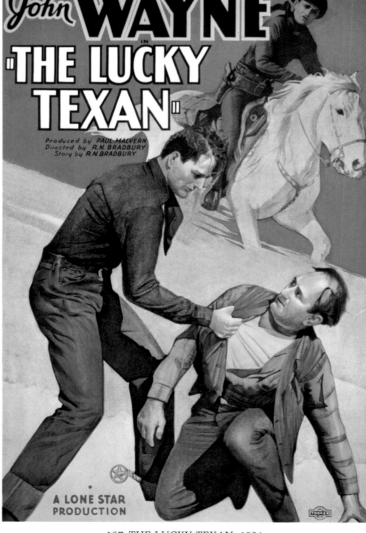

167 THE LUCKY TEXAN, 1934

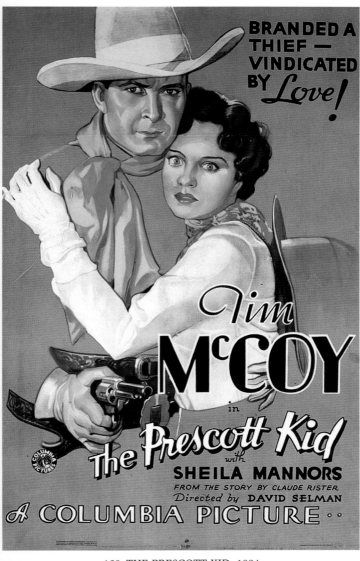

168 THE PRESCOTT KID, 1934

169 WHEN A MAN SEES RED, 1934

170 THE FIGHTING CODE, 1934

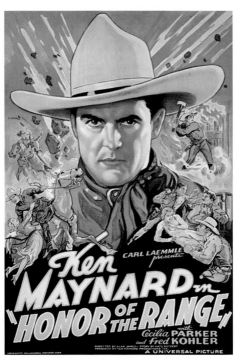

171 HONOR OF THE RANGE, 1934

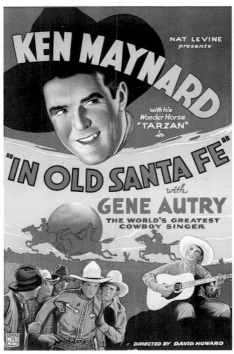

172 IN OLD SANTA FE, 1934

173 HOP-A-LONG CASSIDY, 1935, three-sheet, 81 × 41 in

174 HOP-A-LONG CASSIDY, 1935, six-sheet, 81 × 81 in

175 THE EAGLE'S BROOD, 1935

176 THE IVORY-HANDLED GUN, 1935

177 THE IVORY-HANDLED GUN, 1935, three-sheet, 81 × 41 in

178 THE SINGING VAGABOND, 1935,
three-sheet, 81 × 41 in

179 THE PHANTOM EMPIRE, 1935

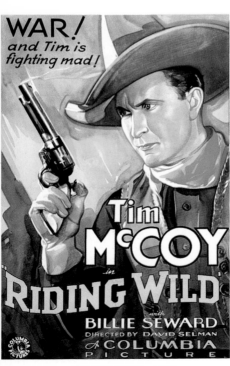

180 RIDING WILD, 1935

181 THE SINGING VAGABOND, 1935

182 THE PHANTOM EMPIRE, 1935, three-sheet, 81 × 41 in

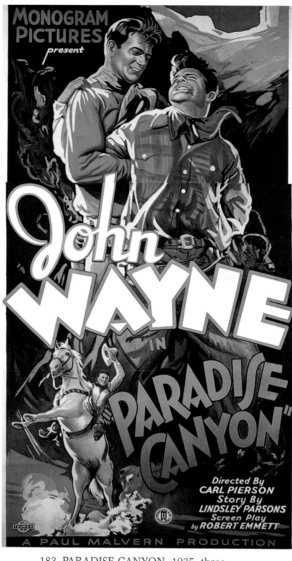

183 PARADISE CANYON, 1935, three-
sheet, 81 × 41 in

184 THE NEW FRONTIER, 1935

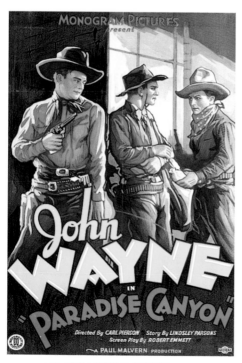

185 PARADISE CANYON, 1935

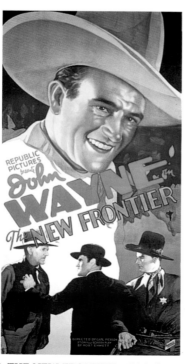

186 THE NEW FRONTIER, 1935, three-
sheet, 81 × 41 in

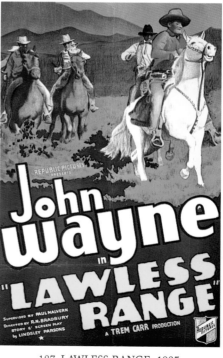

187 LAWLESS RANGE, 1935

In the early thirties, someone in a studio's marketing department came up with the idea of a double feature. A major or "A" picture was paired with a lesser or "B" film. Most of the Westerns of the thirties were produced as B pictures. In the midst of the Great Depression, the studios began to cut back production of the double features, and the Western film began to decline in popularity. Major shuffling of studio personnel and movie actors occurred, and independent studios came and went overnight.

Ken Maynard jumped from Tiffany to World Wide to Mascot to Universal, all in the span of three years. Buck Jones left Columbia for Universal in 1934. Tim McCoy left Columbia to join the independents in 1935, never to star for a major film studio again.

The works of author Zane Grey served as excellent source material for the Western film. Victor Fleming had made a series of films based on the Grey novels in the twenties. In the early thirties, Paramount decided to produce sound remakes of these silent films. Much of the old footage was edited into the new films, giving them an epic look on a small budget. Newcomer Randolph Scott starred in this very successful series, along with Western greats Harry Carey, Larry (Buster) Crabbe, Raymond Hatton, Big-Boy Williams, and screen villain Noah Beery.

In 1933, John Wayne appeared in the first of many low-budget quickies for Monogram, working with famous cowboy sidekick, George Hayes. Hayes played everything from crotchety sheriffs to outlaw leaders. Wayne also began a long association with stunt man, and silent film cowboy, Yakima Canutt. Canutt is credited with helping Wayne develop his stylized walk. Together, they revolutionized the art of screen fist fights.

In 1935, Paramount made the first in the long-running series of 66 Hopalong Cassidy films. William Boyd starred as the silver-haired, black-clad hero. Fresh from the John Wayne Monogram series, George Hayes costarred as Windy Halliday, Hoppy's cantankerous but lovable old sidekick. When Hayes left the series, producer Pop Sherman wouldn't permit his use of the 'Windy' moniker, so Hayes became 'Gabby.' During his lengthy career, he played opposite Ken Maynard, Buck Jones, Tim McCoy, John Wayne, Wild Bill Elliot, Randolph Scott, and Roy Rogers. In the fifties, William Boyd purchased the rights to the Cassidy films in order to release them to television. Hoppy found a new audience and, by licensing toys and games with the Hopalong Cassidy name, Boyd became one wealthy cowpoke.

There was little doubt about what you would see in a Gene Autry picture. With titles like *Yodelin' Kid From Pine Ridge, Rootin' Tootin' Rhythm,* and *Guns And Guitars,* you knew you were in store for a lot of music with a little shooting thrown in to boot. Autry was the only cowboy to always portray himself on the screen; his only role was Gene Autry.

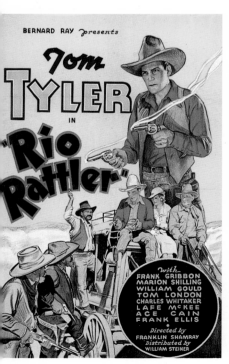

188 RIO RATTLER, 1935

189 ROCKY MOUNTAIN MYSTERY, 1935

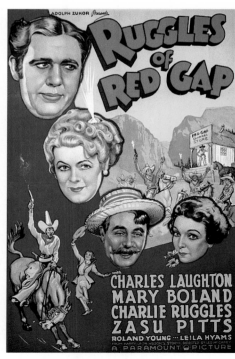

190 RUGGLES OF RED GAP, 1935

191 THE SINGING COWBOY, 1936, three-sheet, 81 × 41 in

194 OH, SUSANNA!, 1936

192 RED RIVER VALLEY, 1936, three-sheet, 81 × 41 in

195 THE VIGILANTES ARE COMING, EPISODE 2, 1936

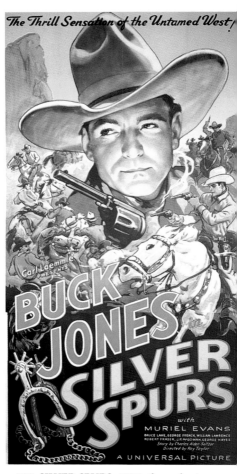

193 SILVER SPURS, 1936, three-sheet, 81 × 41 in

196 THE BOSS RIDER OF GUN CREEK, 1936

197 KING OF THE PECOS, 1936, three-sheet, 81 × 41 in

198 KING OF THE PECOS, 1936

199 WINDS OF THE WASTELAND, 1936, three-sheet, 81 × 41 in

200 THE OREGON TRAIL, 1936

201 THE LONELY TRAIL, 1936

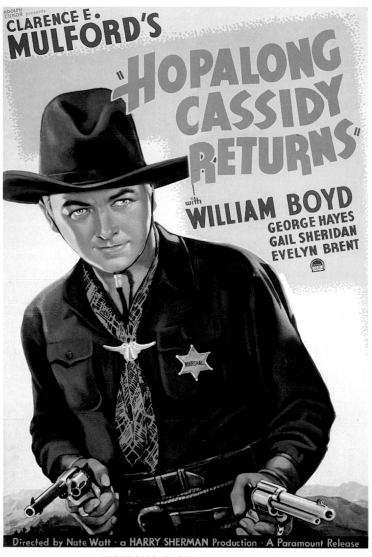

202 HOPLONG CASSIDY RETURNS, 1936

203 RIDE 'EM COWBOY, 1936, three-sheet, 81 × 41 in

204 RAMONA, 1936

205 NEVADA, 1936, three-sheet, 81 × 41 in

206 TREACHERY RIDES THE RANGE, 1936

In 1935, the restructuring of Monogram and Mascot Studios resulted in the formation of Republic Pictures. John Wayne was growing more adept at playing John Wayne and his performances in Republic films, such as *The New Frontier,* and *Winds Of The Wasteland,* clearly showed that he had been working on more than his fast draw.

In 1938, Autry starred in *The Old Barn Dance.* In the cast was a newcomer billed as Dick Weston, whose real name was Leonard Slye. Around this time, Autry entered into a contract dispute with Republic Pictures. He was the biggest buckaroo at the box office and believed he should be paid accordingly. When Republic failed to meet Autry's salary demands, he walked out and in rode Leonard Slye, King of the Cowboys, who would go on to fame as Roy Rogers. Republic put everything they had into building the image of their new warbler. Rogers' career took off, and he continued to make films into the fifties when he began his own television series. Autry eventually worked out his differences with Republic and made many very successful films for the studio.

Some of Hollywood's mainstream actors began appearing in Westerns. Jimmy Stewart first donned a pair of spurs in the 1939 classic *Destry Rides Again,* teaming with dance hall girl Marlene Dietrich. Joel McCrea had been around Hollywood since the silent days and, while appearing in a wide variety of films, he is most often associated with the Western. Filmmaker Cecil B. DeMille starred McCrea in his railroad epic of 1939, *Union Pacific.*

Top adventure film star Errol Flynn appeared in several Westerns, beginning in 1939 with the lavish color film *Dodge City.* The film was a box-office success, and though Flynn seemed more at home with a sword, he did strap on a six-gun again in the forties. Henry Fonda appeared in *Drums Along The Mohawk* and co-starred as outlaw Frank James opposite Tyrone Power (in the title role) in 1939's *Jesse James.* It was a big stretch for tough guy James Cagney to play a swaggering cowboy in Warner Brothers' *The Oklahoma Kid.* To help him feel more at home on the range, arch-nemesis Humphrey Bogart was cast as the villain. Though the film was well done, both actors quickly headed back to the big city.

Singing cowpoke Tex Ritter began making films in 1936, giving Gene Autry a run for his money at the box office. Ritter's film career wound down in the forties, while his music became more popular. Today he is perhaps best remembered for his crooning of the *High Noon* theme song.

In 1939, John Ford assembled a top-notch cast, including Claire Trevor, Tom Tyler, Andy Devine, and Thomas Mitchell, to make what many people consider *the* classic Western, *Stagecoach.* John Wayne was more than ready for the role that would make him a major star — outlaw Johnny Ringo.

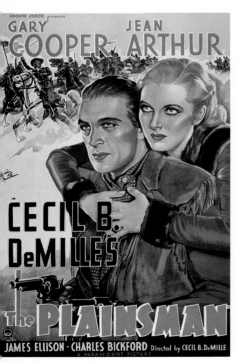

207 THE PLAINSMAN, 1937

208 THE PLAINSMAN, 1937

209 THE PLAINSMAN, 1937, original French poster, 63 × 47 in

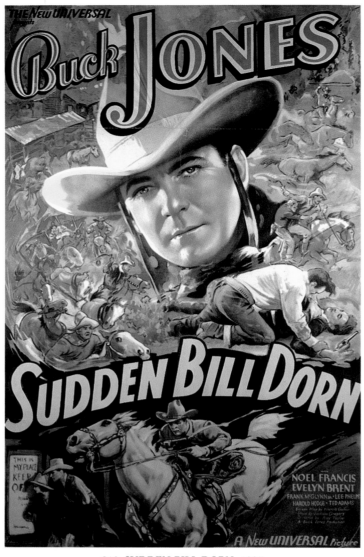

210 SUDDEN BILL DORN, 1937

211 BLACK ACES, 1937

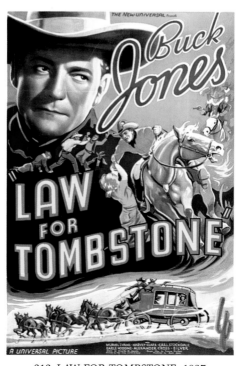

212 LAW FOR TOMBSTONE, 1937

213 HOLLYWOOD ROUNDUP, 1937

214 WELLS FARGO, 1937

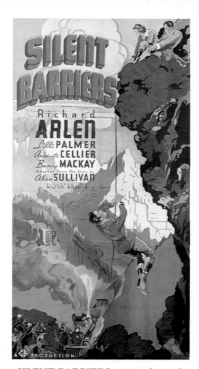

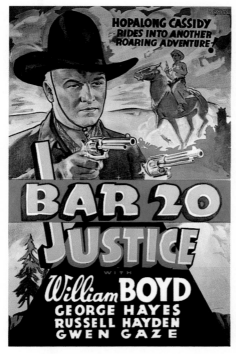

215 PUBLIC COWBOY NO. 1, 1937, three-sheet, 81 × 41 in

216 SILENT BARRIERS, 1937, three-sheet, 81 × 41 in

217 BAR 20 JUSTICE, 1938, "other company"

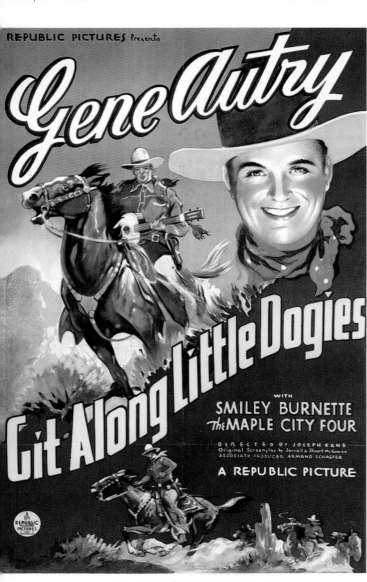

218 GIT ALONG LITTLE DOGIES, 1937

219 BAR 20 JUSTICE, 1938

220 ARIZONA DAYS, 1937, three-sheet, 81 × 41 in

221 THUNDER TRAIL, 1937, three-sheet, "other company," 81 × 41 in

222 WILD AND WOOLLY, 1937, three-sheet, 81 × 41 in

223 TROUBLE IN TEXAS, 1937

224 THUNDER TRAIL, 1937, "other company"

225 RECKLESS RANGER, 1937

226 UNDER WESTERN STARS, 1938

227 THE TEXANS, 1938

228 THE TEXANS, 1938, "other company"

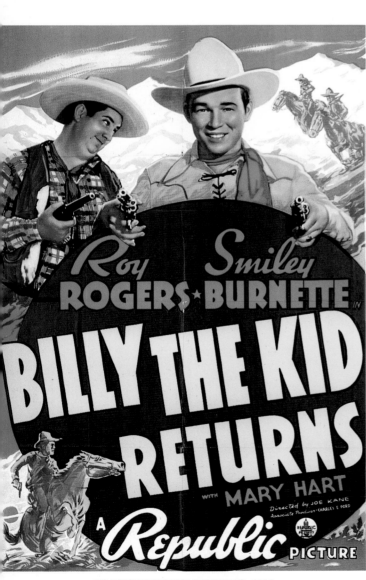

229 BILLY THE KID RETURNS, 1938

230 HEART OF ARIZONA, 1938, three-
sheet, 81 × 41 in

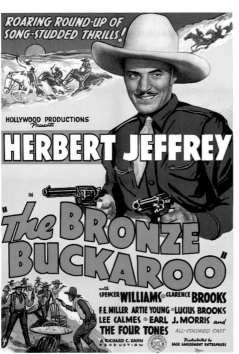

231 THE BRONZE BUCKAROO, 1938

232 SONGS AND BULLETS, 1938

233 THE LONE RANGER, EPISODE 13, 1938

234 HARLEM ON THE PRAIRIE, 1938, three-sheet, 81 × 41 in

235 RAWHIDE, 1938, half-sheet, 22 × 28 in

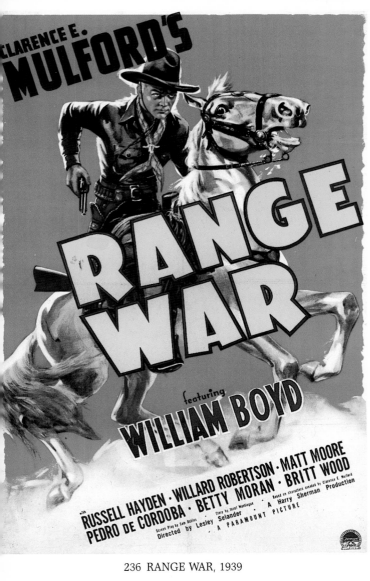

236 RANGE WAR, 1939

237 THE ARIZONA KID, 1939

238 SILVER ON THE SAGE, 1939

239 SAGA OF DEATH VALLEY, 1939

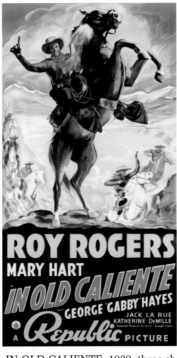

240 IN OLD CALIENTE, 1939, three-sheet,
81 × 41 in

241 THE OKLAHOMA KID, 1939, original
Italian poster, 55 × 39 in

242 THE OKLAHOMA KID, 1939, three-
sheet, "other company," 81 × 41 in

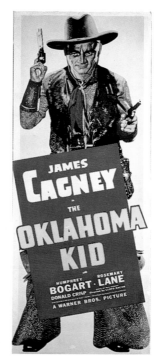

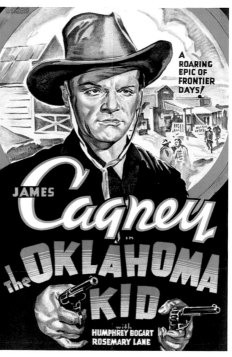

243 THE OKLAHOMA KID, 1939, insert,
36 × 14 in

244 THE OKLAHOMA KID, 1939, "other
company"

245 THE OKLAHOMA KID, 1939

246 STAGECOACH, 1939, original French
poster, 63 × 47 in

247 STAGECOACH, 1939, half-sheet,
22 × 28 in

248 STAGECOACH, 1939, original French
poster, 63 × 47 in

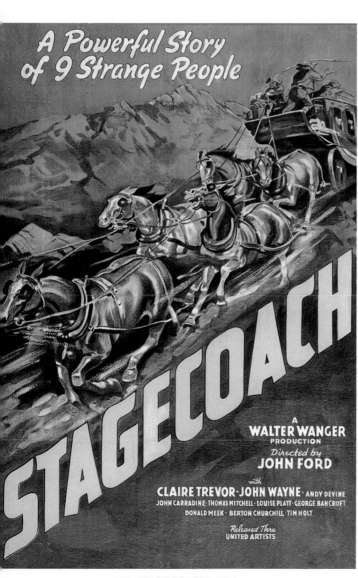

249 STAGECOACH, 1939

250 STAGECOACH, 1939, original Italian
poster, 55 × 39 in

251 JESSE JAMES, 1939, original French
poster, 63 × 47 in

252 DODGE CITY, 1939

253 UNION PACIFIC, 1939

254 DRUMS ALONG THE MOHAWK,
1939

255 DESTRY RIDES AGAIN, 1939

256 BRIGHAM YOUNG, 1940

257 SANTA FE TRAIL, 1940

258 THE WESTERNER, 1940, original Argentinian poster, 44 × 29 in

the forties

When major Hollywood stars began appearing in Westerns, it elevated their usual B status to A and attracted audiences not usually interested in the genre. Color and sex added to the mix resulted in the most popular time in the history of the Western, the forties.

Eccentric millionaire and RKO Studio owner Howard Hughes put protege Jane Russell on all of the posters advertising the 1941 film, *The Outlaw.* The film dealt with the Pat Garrett, Doc Holliday, Billy the Kid relationships, but the full-figured Jane Russell attracted all of the attention. The board of censors held up the film's release pending a decision on how to properly handle Miss Russell and the film's eroticism.

A huge budget and major star power couldn't duplicate the success of *Gone With The Wind* for producer David O. Selznick. *Duel In The Sun,* starring Gregory Peck, Jennifer Jones, Lionel Barrymore, Lillian Gish, and Joseph Cotton, was an entertaining, if overwrought, Western soap opera.

German director Fritz Lang was called to direct *The Return Of Frank James* in 1940. Henry Fonda returned in the title role and went on to star in four more classic westerns of the decade. The first was John Ford's dark tale of mistaken frontier justice, *The Ox-Bow Incident.* Second came Ford's *My Darling Clementine,* Fonda playing town-taming marshal Wyatt Earp. Roles in *Fort Apache* and *The Tin Star* finished out the decade.

Tall and lanky Gary Cooper began his career as a Paramount Studio stunt rider and extra. In his role as *The Virginian,* Cooper played the thoughtful, soft-spoken character he would become identified with in later years. He ran up against Walter Brennan's ruthless Judge Roy Bean in *The Westerner.* Brennan had appeared in Westerns since 1927, turning up in many of the Tim McCoy Columbias of the thirties and playing Old Man Clanton in *My Darling Clementine.* His wide range of character roles included frontier doctors, lovable old codgers, and evil killers.

Robert Mitchum, who had tangled with Hopalong Cassidy in several pictures, appeared in two offbeat Westerns of the forties. Film noir was very popular at the time, and the darkly lit interiors and desperate characters, unique to that genre, were adapted to the Western in *Pursued* and *Blood On The Moon.*

After loaning the services of John Wayne to United Artists for *Stagecoach,* Republic wasted no time in making the most of their rising star. *Dark Command* was rushed into production and costarred his *Stagecoach* love interest Claire Trevor. Wayne appeared in one high-calibre cowboy picture after another: *The Spoilers* (with Randolph Scott and Marlene Dietrich), *In Old California, Tall In The Saddle* (a favorite of Wayne fans), *War Of The Wildcats,* and the classic *Angel And The Badman.* In 1947 Wayne began his association with director Howard Hawks. Their first film effort resulted in the classic *Red River.* Ford called on him again to star in *Fort Apache, She Wore A Yellow Ribbon,* and *Three Godfathers.*

259 THE RETURN OF FRANK JAMES,
1940, original Italian poster, 55 × 39 in

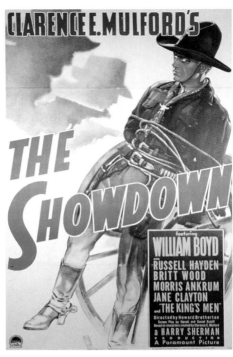

260 THE SHOWDOWN, 1940

261 STAGECOACH WAR, 1940

262 THE MARK OF ZORRO, 1940

263 THE MARK OF ZORRO, 1940, original
Spanish poster, 42 × 28 in

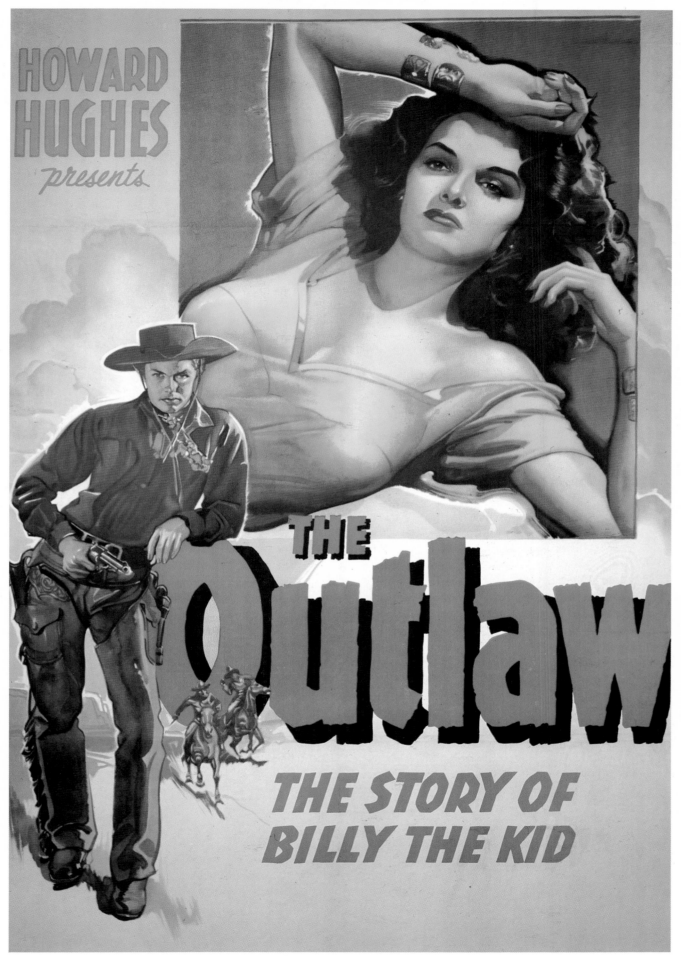

264 THE OUTLAW, 1941

265 BELLE STARR, 1941

266 WESTERN UNION, 1941

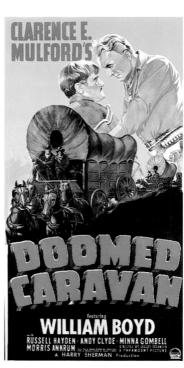

267 RED RIVER VALLEY, 1941

268 DOOMED CARAVAN, 1941, three-sheet, 81 × 41 in

269 UNDER FIESTA STARS, 1941

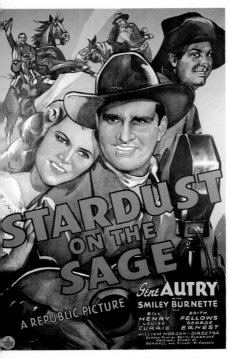

270 STARDUST ON THE SAGE, 1942

271 THE OX-BOW INCIDENT, 1943

272 UTAH, 1945

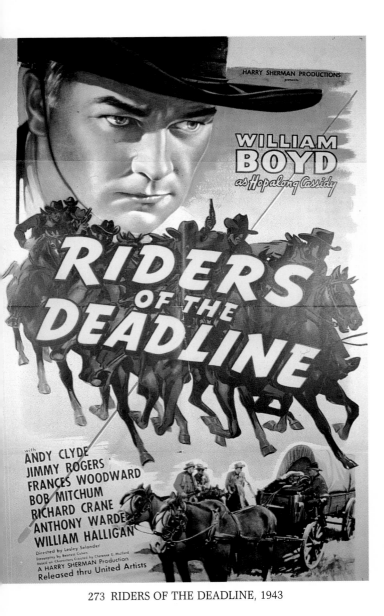

273 RIDERS OF THE DEADLINE, 1943

274 MYSTERY MAN, 1944

275 ALONG CAME JONES, 1945, three-sheet, 81 × 41 in

276 BLACK ARROW, 1944, six-sheet, 81 × 81 in

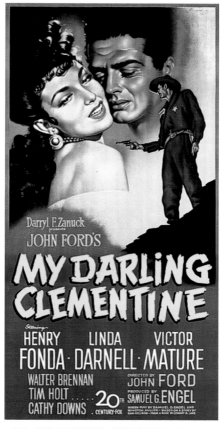

277 DUEL IN THE SUN, 1946, original Italian poster, 55 × 39 in

278 MY DARLING CLEMENTINE, 1946, three-sheet, 81 × 41 in

279 MY DARLING CLEMENTINE, 1946

280 PURSUED, 1947, original Italian
poster, 55 × 39 in

281 RED RIVER, 1948, original Italian
poster, 55 × 39 in

282 COLORADO TERRITORY, 1949,
original Italian poster, 55 × 39 in

283 SHE WORE A YELLOW RIBBON,
1949

284 SHE WORE A YELLOW RIBBON,
1949, original Italian poster, 55 × 39 in

the fifties

By the 1950s the old studio system of film-making was rapidly decaying. Television was cutting down on theater attendance, so film-makers introduced Technicolor, 3-D, and CinemaScope to entice people back to the big screen. Assembly-line Westerns were a thing of the past. Outdoor extravaganzas were still being made, but there was a growing trend toward more introspective or psychological Westerns.

In 1950, Director Henry King made the down-beat *The Gunfighter,* the tale of doomed gunman Gregory Peck. The film set the stage for many of the bleak films that would follow.

Stanley Kramer's 1952 film, *High Noon,* has garnered a classic reputation over time. The abandoned sheriff, Will Kane, was one of Gary Cooper's last and greatest roles.

In 1952, George Stevens directed Alan Ladd in *Shane,* another classic look at Western morals and the changing frontier. The film is full of

memorable images that have secured its classic stature – sadistic badman Jack Palance literally blowing Elisha Cook off his feet with a gunshot, and child actor Brandon De Wilde calling after Ladd, "Shane, come back" at the film's conclusion.

In the early fifties, John Wayne formed his own production company. One of its first films, *Hondo,* cashed in on the 3-D craze. Three years later, Wayne would play anti-hero Ethan Edwards in the 1956 *The Searchers.* This is often considered John Wayne's greatest film role and was his personal favorite, inspiring him to name one of his sons, Ethan.

In 1955, Walt Disney Studios made a star out of Fess Parker and a household word out of frontiersman Davy Crockett. So popular was Crockett's hat that its mass merchandising nearly caused the extinction of the raccoon. *Davy Crockett* was a sensation and prompted the studio's resurrection of Zorro and other western heroes.

285 STAGE TO TUCSON, 1950, three-sheet, 81 × 41 in

286 THE GUNFIGHTER, 1950, original Italian poster, 55 × 39 in

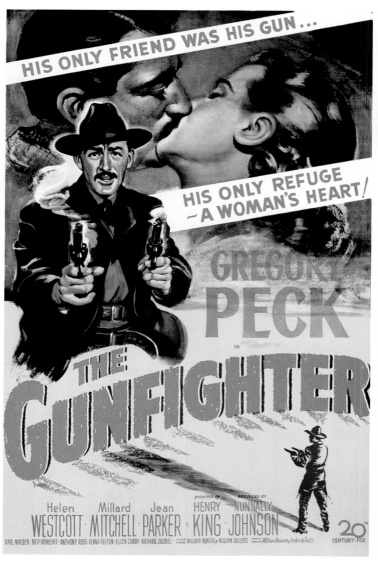

287 THE GUNFIGHTER, 1950

288 RIO GRANDE, 1950, original Italian
poster, 55 × 39 in

289 WINCHESTER '73, 1950, original
Italian poster, 55 × 39 in

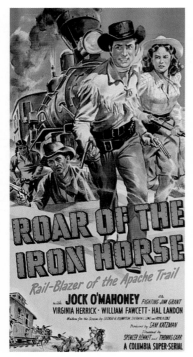

290 ROAR OF THE IRON HORSE, 1951,
three-sheet, 81 × 41 in

291 THE LUSTY MEN, 1952, original
Italian poster, 55 × 39 in

292 RANCHO NOTORIOUS, 1952, original
Italian poster, 55 × 39 in

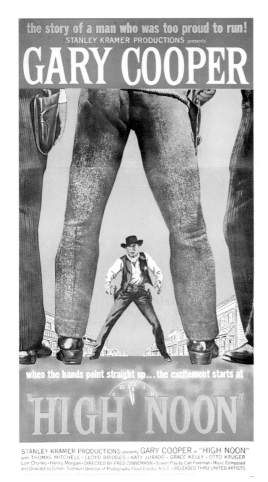

293 HIGH NOON, 1952, three-sheet,
81 × 41 in

294 HIGH NOON, 1952, half-sheet,
22 × 28 in

295 HIGH NOON, 1952, original Italian
poster, 55 × 39 in

296 LAW AND ORDER, 1953

297 SHANE, 1953, three-sheet,
81 × 41 in

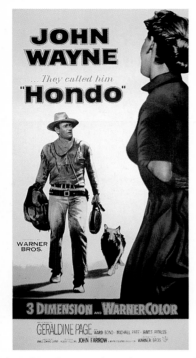

298 HONDO, 1954, three-sheet, 81 × 41 in

299 JESSE JAMES' WOMEN, 1954

300 THE MAN FROM LARAMIE, 1955

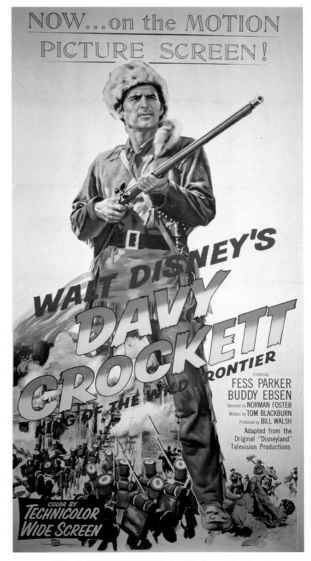

301 HONDO, 1954, original Italian poster,
55 × 39 in

302 DAVY CROCKETT, 1955, three-sheet,
81 × 41 in

303 THE SEARCHERS, 1956, original
Belgian poster, 22 × 14 in

304 RIDE LONESOME, 1959, original
Italian poster, 55 × 39 in

305 THE TALL T, 1957, original Italian
poster, 55 × 39 in

306 THE SHERIFF OF FRACTURED JAW,
1958, original Italian poster, 55 × 39 in

307 MAN OF THE WEST, 1958

the sixties

The traditional values put forth in the early Western were buried on Boot Hill by the time the sixties arrived. The clear-cut good versus evil themes were replaced by films where the good guys were outlaws, and the entire cast often planted six feet under by the time the end credits rolled by.

The Alamo completely disregarded the current trend toward realism. John Wayne produced, directed and starred as Davy Crockett in this bleached-white historical epic. In 1962, Wayne was *The Man Who Shot Liberty Valance,* and, in 1969, he won an Oscar for his role in *True Grit.*

Many big stars made even bigger Westerns. Marlon Brando directed and starred in *One-Eyed Jacks.* Yul Brynner, Steve McQueen, James Coburn, and Charles Bronson joined forces in *The Magnificent Seven.* William Holden, Ernest Borgnine and Robert Ryan starred in Sam Peckinpah's ultraviolent *The Wild Bunch.* Clark Gable, Montgomery Clift and Marilyn Monroe starred in *The Misfits,* John Huston's contemporary Western. Paul Newman and Robert Redford were *Butch Cassidy And The Sundance Kid.*

In 1964, a new genre was born, the Spaghetti Western, referring to its country of origin, Italy. Director Sergio Leone and star, Clint Eastwood, became internationally famous with the release of *A Fistful of Dollars, For A Few Dollars More,* and *The Good, The Bad and The Ugly.*

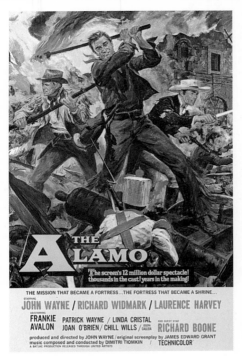

308 THE ALAMO, 1960

309 THE UNFORGIVEN, 1960

310 THE MANIFICIENT SEVEN, 1960,
original Italian poster, 55 × 39 in

311 THE MISFITS, 1961, original Spanish
poster, 42 × 28 in

312 ONE EYED JACKS, 1961, original
Spanish poster, 42 × 28 in

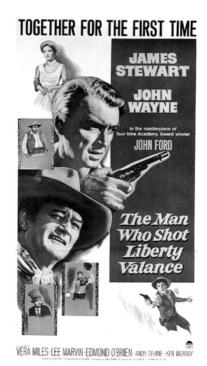

313 THE MAN WHO SHOT LIBERTY
VALENCE, 1962, three-sheet, 81 × 41 in

314 INVITATION TO A GUNFIGHTER,
1964

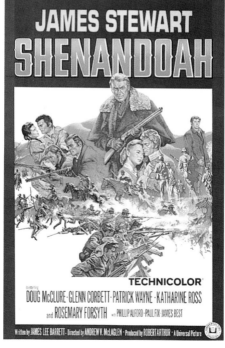

315 SHENANDOAH, 1965

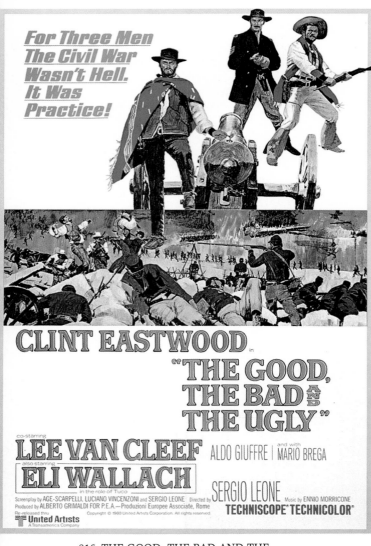

316 THE GOOD, THE BAD AND THE
UGLY, 1966

317 FOR A FEW DOLLAR MORE, 1965,
original Italian poster, 55 × 39 in

318 ALVAREZ KELLY, 1966

319 THE RARE BREED, 1966

320 KILLER ON A HORSE, 1967

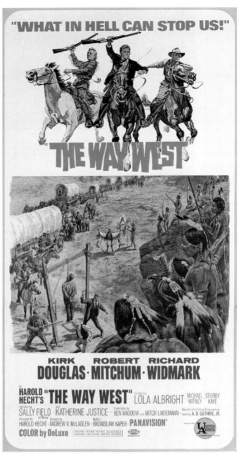

321 THE WAY WEST, 1967, three-sheet,
81 × 41 in

322 BUTCH CASSIDY AND THE SUN-
DANCE KID, 1969, half-sheet, 22 × 28 in

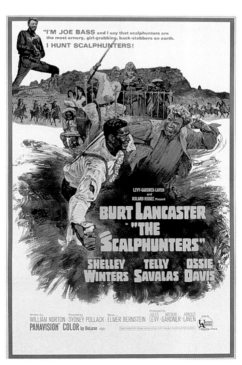

323 THE SCALPHUNTERS, 1968

324 BANDOLERO, 1968

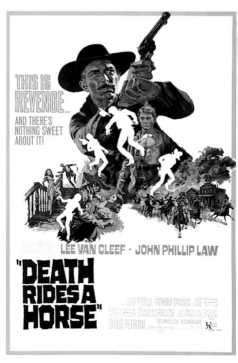

325 DEATH RIDES A HORSE, 1968

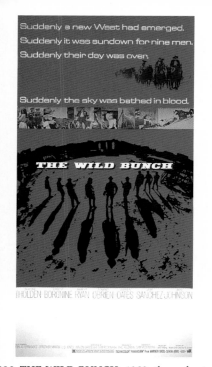

326 THE WILD BUNCH, 1969, three-sheet, 81 × 41 in

327 DAY OF ANGER, 1969

328 ONCE UPON A TIME IN THE WEST, 1969

329 PAINT YOUR WAGON, 1969, original Italian poster, 55 × 39 in

330 ONCE UPON A TIME IN THE WEST, 1969, original Italian poster, 55 × 39 in

the seventies

The seventies saw the passing of most of the Western film greats... John Wayne, John Ford, Tim McCoy, William Boyd, Randolph Scott, and Howard Hawks, to name a few. Most of these men had a personal connection to the real West, while new Western filmmakers, however, only had the Hollywood Western as a guide.

Clint Eastwood, who has had more effect on the Westerns of the last 30 years than any other performer, began his career in Westerns as Rowdy Yates on television's "Rawhide". Continuing with variations on the soft-spoken, man-of-mystery character he created in the 60's Spaghetti Westerns, Eastwood appeared in *Hang 'Em High, Joe Kidd,* and *High Plains Drifter,* which he also directed. In 1976, he made *Bronco Billy* as well as starring in and directing *The Outlaw Josey Wales.* This film is widely considered his finest work.

Director Arthur Penn's *Little Big Man* took a look at the taming of the West through the eyes of Native American Dustin Hoffman. Marlon Brando and Jack Nicholson starred in Penn's next film, the bizarre and underrated *The Missouri Breaks.*

Sam Peckinpah made his final Western in 1973, *Pat Garrett and Billy the Kid.* Paul Newman appeared in *The Life And Times Of Judge Roy Bean.* Gene Hackman made the offbeat *Bite The Bullet,* and John Wayne played a gunman dying of cancer in *The Shootist,* his final film.

Current trends toward science fiction prompted the making of *Westworld,* with Yul Brynner as a robotic recreation of his *The Magnificent Seven* gunman.

331 McCABE AND MRS. MILLER, 1971, original French poster, 63 × 47 in

332 DIRTY DINGUS MAGEE, 1970

333 THE LEGEND OF FRENCHIE KING, 1971

334 THE COWBOYS, 1972, three-sheet, 81 × 41 in

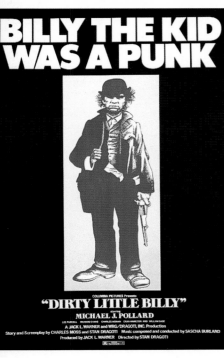

335 DIRTY LITTLE BILLY, 1972

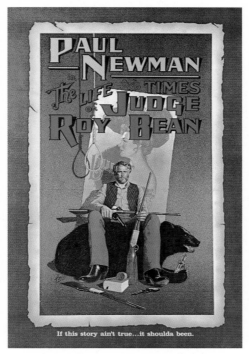

336 THE LIFE AND TIMES OF JUDGE
ROY BEAN, 1972

337 CHINO, 1973

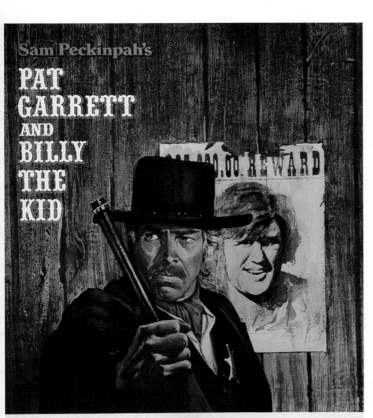

338 PAT GARRETT AND BILLY THE KID,
1973

339 HIGH PLAINS DRIFTER, 1973

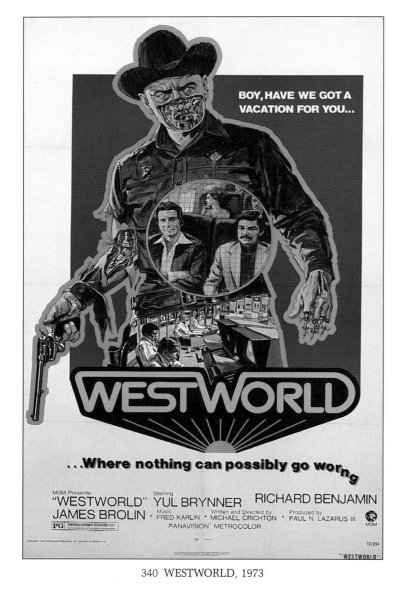

340 WESTWORLD, 1973

341 BITE THE BULLET, 1975

342 RANCHO DELUXE, 1974

343 BUFFALO BILL AND THE INDIANS,
1976

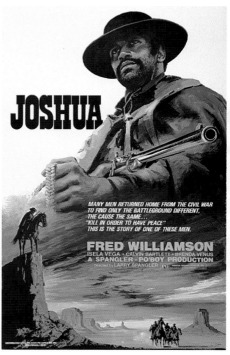

344 JOSHUA, 1976

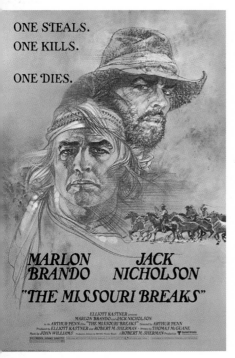

345 THE MISSOURI BREAKS, 1976

346 THE MISSOURI BREAKS, 1976, original Polish poster, 32 × 23 in

347 THE OUTLAW JOSEY WALES, 1976

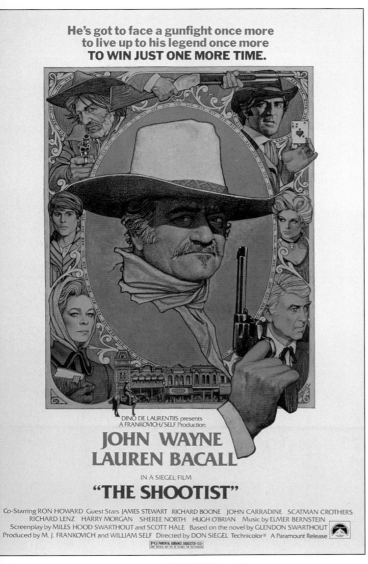

348 THE SHOOTIST, 1976

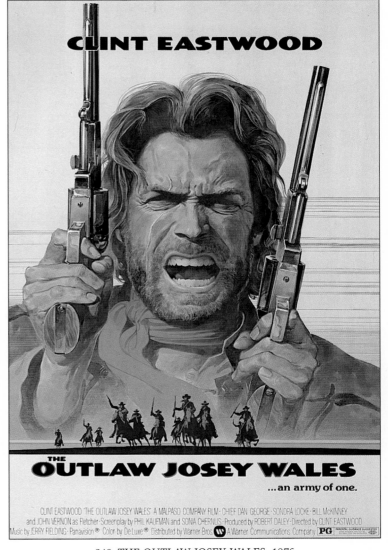

349 THE OUTLAW JOSEY WALES, 1976

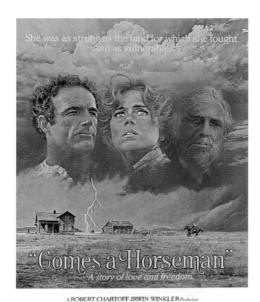

350 ANOTHER MAN, ANOTHER CHANCE, 1977

351 COMES A HORSEMAN, 1978

352 THE LEGEND OF THE LONE RANGER, 1980

the eighties and nineties

Director Michael Cimino of *The Deer Hunter* fame erected a temporary road block for the Western in 1980 with his infamous *Heaven's Gate.* The film's overindulgences could have sounded a death knoll for cowboy tales in this new era. But true to form, the ever-enduring genre picked itself up, dusted itself off, and started all over again.

Walter Hill tackled the Jesse James legend in *The Long Riders.* Writer and director Lawrence Kasdan made *Silverado,* introducing actor Kevin Costner to the Western. Costner directed and starred in the Oscar-winning 1990 film, *Dances With Wolves,* and, in 1994, none-too-successfully rehashed the legend of *Wyatt Earp.* James Garner, who starred in the popular sixties television series *Maverick,* had a supporting role in the big

screen adaptation, which starred Mel Gibson in the title role.

The *Pale Rider* of Clint Eastwood's 1985 film is a mysterious, ghostlike stranger who rescues the inhabitants of a mining town. In 1993, he directed and starred in *The Unforgiven,* a moral tale of a retired gunman. Both films won accolades from the public and critics and successfully captured a younger generation of filmgoers. *The Unforgiven* secured Oscars for best picture and direction.

The nineties roll on with a new generation enjoying the Western on videotape and television. The keen interest in cowboy style, America's frontier history, and Western memorabilia are sure-fire signs of America's never-ending love affair with the cowboy.

353 BRONCO BILLY, 1980

354 HEAVEN'S GATE, 1980

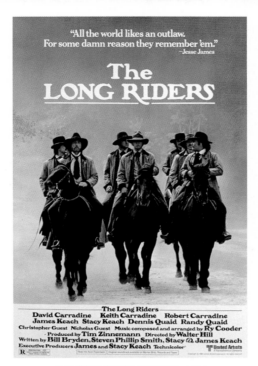

355 THE LONG RIDERS, 1980

356 BARBAROSA, 1982

357 PALE RIDER, 1985

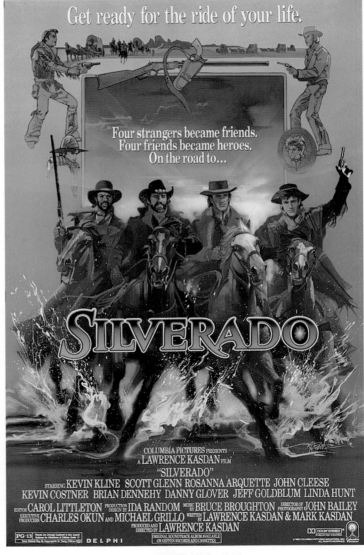

358 SILVERADO, 1985

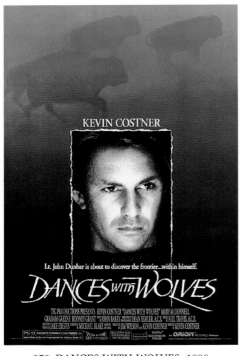

359 DANCES WITH WOLVES, 1990

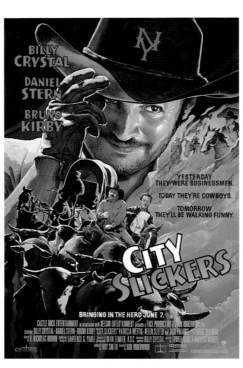

360 CITY SLICKERS, 1991

361 UNFORGIVEN, 1992

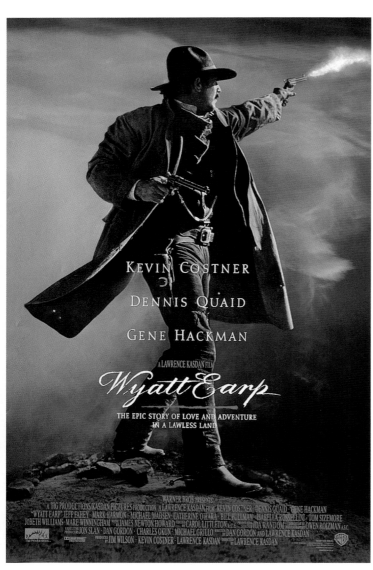

362 WYATT EARP, 1994

363 MAVERICK, 1994

COWBOY MOVIE POSTERS INDEX